BRITAIN IN OLD PHOTOGRAPHS

WILLESDEN

ADAM SPENCER

LONDON BOROUGH OF BRENT

SUTTON PUBLISHING LIMITED

Sutton Publishing Limited
Phoenix Mill · Thrupp · Stroud
Gloucestershire · GL5 2BU

First published 1996

Cover photographs: *front*: Crown Inn,
Harlesden; *back*: first tramcar to Willesden,
7 October 1909.

British Library Cataloguing in Publication Data
A catalogue record for this book is available from the
British Library.

ISBN 0-7509-1171-9

Typeset in 10/12 Perpetua.
Typesetting and origination by
Sutton Publishing Limited.
Printed in Great Britain by
Ebenezer Baylis, Worcester

> Dedicated, with love, to
> Louise and Anne
> Adam Spencer, October 1996

A view of the fields to the south of the Welsh Harp (*see* p.10), *c.* 1920. This picture was taken during the summer months when there were a number of magnificent elm trees in leaf. Since the development of the area for industry and housing the trees have, sadly, long since disappeared. A scene from the surprisingly recent rural past.

CONTENTS

A picture of a tranquil River Brent in the pre-combustion engine era. This photograph, taken near Stonebridge Park in 1921, is close to the aqueduct that carries the Grand Junction Canal over the Brent. This area is now much more closely associated with tarmac than trees and water, as some of the river was covered over in 1934 when the North Circular Road was built.

INTRODUCTION

Willesden parish is roughly triangular in shape and has for its boundaries the Edgware Road to the north east, earlier known as Watling Street, the River Brent to the north and west, and for much of its southern borders, the Harrow Road. The land rises from 30 m along the River Brent to 73 m at Dollis Hill and 75 m at Mount Pleasant, which is on the Brondesbury Ridge. Willesden lies on London clay with Taplow Gravel along the course of the river, with some glacial gravel at Dollis Hill and Claygate Beds at Mount Pleasant. Generally the soils are heavy and the poorly-drained clays were, as the Victoria County History states: 'probably once covered by thick oak forest and well adapted to the grass farming that characterized the area from the 18th century'.

Aside from the Roman legacy of Watling Street, there is little evidence of man's activities in the Willesden area – indeed some writers have referred to evidence of a settlement before the Saxons as 'dubious'. What is apparent is that from the Anglo-Saxon era hamlets were established in woodland clearings on well-drained sites near streams or wells, such as Willesden Green, Neasden and Harlesden. By 1000 the whole of the parish was in the possession of St Paul's Cathedral. Prebendal estates were then established. Prior to the Reformation, Willesden was most popularly associated with the shrine to Our Lady and in 1297 the church of St Mary's was described as being 'consecrated in honour of the Blessed Mary'. It was around the time of the plague that the shrine began to become famous as a place of pilgrimage. Essentially the settlement pattern of the parish altered very little between the Middle Ages and the middle of the nineteenth century, the parish having undergone enclosure in 1816.

The 1801 census for Willesden, gave a figure of just 98 houses, which is considered by most commentators to be too low. There were 178 houses by the 1811 census, 254 in 1821 and 358 by 1831. At this stage the parish was still regarded as a place of rural tranquillity. However, in the mid-1800s things began to change as the proximity of Willesden to the growing metropolis had its effect: 'The outward expansion of the metropolis reached Willesden in the mid-19th century, when there were 578 houses in Willesden, engulfing South Kilburn in the 1850s and 1860s and north Kilburn in the 1870s and 1880s. Proceeding along Harrow Road, it affected Kensal Green and Harlesden, whose growth was also stimulated by the building of Willesden Junction station just outside the borders. The first entirely new developments, at Brondesbury and Stonebridge from the 1860s and 1870s respectively, took place in estates bordering main roads and served by the railway.'

From then on there was a continuous demand for new housing, and this particular stage of development did not run its course until well within living memory, when the northerly parts of the parish were built on in the 1930s. Development was haphazard. Large developers like the United Land Company, All Souls College and the Ecclesiastical Commissioners tried to reign in some of the worst aspects of speculative building, but there were still many problems, typified by the houses built in Kilburn that were isolated among unmade-up roads. By 1890 it had become obvious that the parish could not sustain the middle-class development that had characterized the first wave of new housing. Instead the tendency to build low-cost working-class homes prevailed. This was most clearly to be seen in the residential estates of the railway companies.

In the early 1900s Willesden was essentially residential and the two largest categories of employed men worked in transport and building. There was an economic slump in the pre-First World War period, and in the 1920s the local authorities, anxious to try and avoid the problems of unemployment, encouraged new building. Between 1921 and 1939 the number of houses and flats increased from 24,919 to 42,418. Despite the huge number of new properties built, the population soon outstripped them – population growth between 1921 and 1931 stood at 19 per cent and between 1931 and 1939 it was 13 per cent. Consequently, overcrowding still existed, which the Labour-controlled authority attempted to address in the 1930s. The Second World War made the situation worse – 1,300 houses were destroyed and 6,500 severely damaged. The Willesden Survey of 1947 established that overcrowding, over-industrialization and lack of planning lay at the root of the parish's problems: 'There was little sense of identity or community. Historically Willesden was a parish of separate hamlets and the building of canals, railway and roads like the North Circular had served not to link but to divide them.'

Looking towards Hampstead, *c.* 1880. A picture from F.A. Wood's archive (*see* pp. 35 and 61), this image is taken from the tower of Christchurch, Brondesbury (*see* p. 17) looking over Mapesbury to Shoot-up-Hill and beyond to Hampstead. In the middle distance, two new Victorian villas on the Camden side of the Edgware Road can be seen, heralding the ribbon development of this major road.

WATERWAYS

River Brent, Neasden, 1920. Another charming example of the rural beauty still evident around the wandering course of the River Brent. This photograph shows the river at Neasden, and in conjunction with other photos on pp.1 and 4 helps to evoke the image of a more sedate and tranquil environment.

Two views of the River Brent as it threads its way through Willesden, *c.* 1910. Above is, apparently, Dudden Hill pond, while the photo below shows the Brent, 'near Harlesden'. This was taken for the Kelly's Directories. Brent is one of the few surviving Celtic place names in the district; it means 'holy one' or 'holy river'. There has been some disagreement as to exactly where the upper photograph was taken, Dudden Hill being some way from the river. It is possible that it shows a pond unconnected with the Brent, although the original caption clearly states 'Dudden Hill Pond, River Brent.' Despite the lack of hard evidence the suggested date for both photos is about 1910.

The canal feeder was constructed in about 1809 to help solve the problem of water supply to the Grand Junction Canal (*see* below, pp. 10 and 91). This need for water eventually led to the creation of the Brent Reservoir or Welsh Harp (*see* p. 10). This photograph comes from the lecture on Willesden history presented by Stanley Ball (*see* p. 63) and features Councillor W.R. Dunn and a little boy fishing for sticklebacks, *c*. 1900.

Grand Junction Canal, 1921. One of the very few surviving photographs of activity on the Grand Junction Canal (*see* pp. 10 and 91), this shows a group of young men enjoying a row. It has been suggested that the boat was probably hired from Jack's Cabin, Lower Place.

Grand Junction Canal, *c.* 1910, with the bridge carrying Acton Lane over it, and the side of the Grand Junction Arms on the left. Evidence of the horse-drawn nature of the canal boats can be clearly seen on the towpath. The gentleman standing here was a Willesden Guardian of the Poor named Jimmy Perkins (*see* p. 62). This scene looks much the same in the picture on page 91, so the two photographs must have been taken at about the same time.

The Welsh Harp or Brent Reservoir, *c.* 1920. A picture from a private family album, sadly lacking provenance, which shows part of a seaplane-versus-speedboat race. The speedboat has already gone past the camera. The Welsh Harp has fluctuated in size over the years, varying from between 350 and 400 acres in 1870 to 195.7 acres in 1894 to 176.4 acres in 1914, 150.2 acres in 1935 and 125 acres in 1980.

PLACES OF WORSHIP

St Mary's Willesden, 1844. A very pleasant engraving, taken prior to the Victorian restorations. Note the figures in the foreground in front of the impressive elm tree and by the gate. Also note the mean wooden-framed and truncated east window which replaced the previous masonry and fine tracery.

St Mary's vicarage, *c.* 1900. One of perhaps only two surviving pictures of the 'Holy Well' in St Mary's vicarage garden. The old church can be seen over the wall on the other side of Neasden Lane. The dog probably belongs to Revd James Dixon. A resident of the time said that the pond was fed by a spring and drained away from the centre, causing any toy boats sailed upon it to be sucked in.

St Mary's, c. 1905. The graves with railings in the right foreground belong to the nineteenth century Nicoll family, and were removed for road widening in the late 1950s. Note the restored east window as compared to the print on p.11.

St Mary's from the south with the south porch, just to the right of the tower, hidden by lime trees, which have since been uprooted. The ash tree to the left of the tower, however, is now gigantic.

Church of Our Lady, *c.* 1910. A postcard showing the Roman Catholic Church of Our Lady, in Crownhill Road, Harlesden, adjacent to the Convent of Jesus and Mary. A Mass was said at 6 St Anne's Terrace (now 89 Tubbs Road) on 8 February 1886, and the congregation was such that the erection of the 'Tin Cathedral', a temporary iron structure in Manor Park Road, followed in June 1886. This building, built in 1907, was decorated with Italian terracotta in the Romanesque style, and replaced the temporary church in Manor Park Road.

St Gabriel's, 1900, on Walm Lane opposite the junction of Chichele Road and Melrose Avenue, sometime after being struck by lightning on Friday 27 July 1900, when the roof of the nave was destroyed. The Willesden fire brigade attended to the resulting blaze and Superintendent Edwards was injured by falling slates. The church was designed by W. Bassett Smith and Pochard P. Day between 1896 and 1897. The restoration of the nave took place in 1902–3. The building now consists of a nave, north and south aisles, chancel, north-east chapel and western saddleback tower.

Willesden New Cemetery Chapels, *c.* 1910. They were erected in 1891–2. Charles H. Worley was the architect and Richard Ballard, the contractor. It was decided to have two chapels opening on to an arched entrance way, one for Church of England services, and the other for Nonconformist use. The building is of stock brick with Bath stone facings. It was consecrated by the Bishop of Marlborough on 21 October 1892.

St Andrew's clergy, *c.* 1906. Five priests wearing birettas pose for a photograph outside St Andrew's vicarage, Willesden Green. The central figure is Father Ernest Arundell Morgan, second vicar (1906–24). Two of the others are probably Father W.O.B. Rogers and Father F. Cole Robinson who were assistant priests in 1906. Polishing boots must have been one of the clerical disciplines! St Andrew's is one of the few Willesden churches to have followed the High Church tradition continuously since its consecration.

All Souls, Harlesden, *c.* 1885. This church was Edward Tarver's masterpiece and was erected in 1879.
The photograph is taken from the west end of the nave looking towards the octagon. The nave was built in
1890 but has recently been demolished. Despite these changes, the church now remains much the same as
it was when it was first built. Tarver was in charge of the 1872 restoration of St Mary's, Willesden, and
also built the now demolished St Saviour's at Neasden. Note the unusual gas chandeliers.

Christchurch, Brondesbury, *c.* 1880. Surely one of the most impressive churches in Willesden, Christchurch stands just a few metres from the Edgware Road. In about 1880, the suggested date of this photograph, there was little housing adjacent to the church and it clearly provided an impressive vantage point (*see* p. 6).

The Chapel on the High Road, Willesden, *c.* 1890, with Pound Lane going off to the extreme lower right of the photo. The building is still being used for worship today and is known as the Elim Pentecostal, with 'Church on the High Road, no. 334' written on the wall outside. The area must have been dark at night with just one gas lamp in this length of road.

Willesden Chapel, *c.* 1890. This is the first Nonconformist meeting place established in Willesden and was founded in 1820 by Mr Nodes, whose mother apparently complained of the dearth of 'spiritual food' in Willesden. Mr Nodes agreed to visit on Sundays and read her Burder's *Village Sermons*. Neighbours joined in and the congregation grew, and the chapel was subsequently built.

PUBLIC HOUSES

The Spotted Dog, Willesden Green, c. 1920. This certainly existed by 1762 and was probably referred to as The Dog at Willesden Green in 1751. Note the customers surrounding the greengrocer's barrow on the left.

Stonebridge Park Hotel, *c.* 1890. The Stonebridge Park Hotel was opened in about 1875 next to the Stonebridge Park Estate. It is a two-storey detached building of yellow stock brick with a cast iron canopied loggia over the central bay and porch, and it is one of the few Grade II listed buildings in Brent. The presence of the Harrow Road and the opening of the station on the Midland Line in 1875 provided the impetus necessary for new housing. The estate was originally planned as the Harlesden Park Estate, having been laid out in 1873, and in 1876 the properties were being described as smart new villas for city men. One of the new residents was F.A. Wood whose house Hurworth (*see* p. 35) is one of the few survivors.

The remodelled White Horse in Church Road. This postcard view dates from about 1910. In 1888 this building replaced the old public house of 1860 (*see* p.77). Before licensing in 1860 it was an ale-house and prior to that a post office. It is thought that in about 1843 Mrs Craik, author of *John Halifax, Gentlemen*, lived in a house on the site. Mr Thomas Tilbury secured the contract for the building of the new pub. During the demolition of the old building, some old coins were found and what was apparently the remains of the parish cage which was supposed to have held the highwayman Jack Sheppard before his escape. Items of interest in this picture include the name of the brewery on the pub (Michell & Aldous, a local firm, with a brewery in Kilburn on the High Road), and the horse and cart to the right of the image.

A postcard of the William IV, Harrow Road, Kensal Green, *c.* 1910. Howard Barnard wrote in 1927 in *Notes on News*: 'The William IV public house at the corner of Warfield Road, Kensal Green, is being demolished to make way for more commodious up-to-date premises. Several people have written or spoken to me calling attention to the changes, and some have asked whether my note books contain anything interesting about the house that is now passing. It may perhaps be useful to record that a certain William Hodson was the landlord for many years; and in the fifties of the last century it was the terminus of a two-horse 'bus which was run to London Bridge by a Mr Andrews, whose stables were closely adjacent. In those days the "William the Fourth" had a large bowling green at the back surrounded by summer houses and the hinterland, on which Pember, Buller and Halstow roads were long afterwards built, was then known as the "Back Fields" the "Front Fields" being on the other side of Kilburn Lane.'

The Rising Sun, Harlesden Road, *c.* 1890. Little is known about the establishment of this pub in Harlesden Road, although it was certainly in business by 1872 when Isaac Twyford was the landlord. This is the building which was demolished to make way for the new pub, the plans for which were submitted to the scrutiny of Oscar Claude Robson, Surveyor of the Local Board (*see* p. 62) on 21 May 1895. They were duly passed a week later after A.R. Barker, architect and builder of 11 Buckingham Street, Strand, London had written to Robson: 'I trust you will find the alterations requested shown in the manner which will enable you to pass the plans.'

The White Hart, Willesden, *c.* 1890. This shows the exterior of the weatherboarded structure and the pleasure gardens of the pub at Church Road. The lower photograph gives a lovely indication of a typical Victorian beer garden. In the *Willesden Chronicle* there is a report that the proprietor of the White Hart, Thomas B. Jones, entertained a group of twenty-two North American Indians in 1887, including Red Shirt, the fighting chief of the Sioux nation. They were in London performing in the American Exhibition at Earl's Court, with Buffalo Bill. Apparently 'they were great admirers of mild ale . . . and quaffed the potation with a gusto that would have brought crimson to many old toper's face . . .'

The Case is Altered, High Road, Willesden Green, c. 1890. This is the original building. There has been much debate as to the origin of the name, the most likely conclusion being that, as well as the name of a play, it was a commonly used proverb, punchline and anecdote. The name is not particularly rare. While the pub is old it is not listed in the *Pigot's and Co., Commercial Directory . . . of . . . Middlesex* in 1839. It first appears in the census returns for 1861, when Henry Goode was the landlord, and the premises were described as a beer house. He is also listed in our earliest Kelly's Directory for 1872, as a beer retailer. The pub has recently suffered the fate of many local hostelries – conversion to an Irish theme pub – and is now called Ned Kelly's.

Spotted Dog, Dog Lane, Neasden, c. 1930. The Neasden Spotted Dog was given the name by the Nicoll family in 1767. Licensed premises called The Angel can be traced back to 1751 and as Thomas Nicoll was licensee in 1763, it seems probable that when The Angel disappeared and the Dog or Spotted Dog appeared on licensing lists, they refer to the same premises under a new name. The Twyford family held the licence of the Spotted Dog for most of the Victorian era. Joseph Twyford was licensee at the Willesden Green Spotted Dog (*see* p. 19) for thirty years in the first quarter of the nineteenth century before taking over at the Neasden Dog. He retired in the late 1840s. By 1860 the Neasden pub was being run by George Twyford who handed over to his son George William, in 1891.

Harlesden High Street, *c.* 1890. This exceptional photograph might easily have crept into the transport section as it clearly shows both a horse-tram and a horse-bus, as well as the Royal Oak in the background and the Green Man on the right. Amos Beeson, in his reminiscences of the 1870s, tells how the 'Green Man was a regular stopping place for horse vehicles with its water trough in front and its Tea Gardens with seats and tables for the use of visitors to stay and enjoy the open air whilst having tea and refreshment. A cork tree grew in the garden which was very unusual.'

The original Windmill Inn (built in about 1780), Cricklewood, *c.* 1890. The *Willesden Chronicle*, commenting on this picture in 1915, felt moved to tell its readers: 'Records prove conclusively that the first inn which stood on this spot was from time to time used by Dick Turpin and his compeers of the road, and judging by the illustration it does strike one as just the romantic little place that such gentry favoured in their lawless travels'. The building was enlarged in 1898 prior to rebuilding in about 1900.

FARMS

A lovely photograph of Oxford Farm Diary, High Road, Willesden Green,
depicting rural and agricultural Willesden, c. 1880. The notice in the lower
left window advertises 'Nevill's Wheat Meal Bread'. There is also a name
plate on the building, Willesden Cottage, which fixes its location as in-
between Strode Road and The Case is Altered (see p. 23).

Two views of the rear of Gravel Pit Farm, Neasden, *c.* 1890. The name derives, unsurprisingly, from its proximity to the gravel pits near the River Brent, and it is thought that gravel dug from here was used for the repair of Willesden's roads. In November 1880 the gravel pits were described in sales particulars thus: 'There is a large quantity of the finest Gravel on the Property, which can be very profitably worked, whilst a portion of the land could at once be utilised for building purposes. The whole of the land immediately opposite to this Property has been sold to the Metropolitan Railway, and will probably soon be developed for building purposes, thus giving an additional element to this Land.' Braemar Avenue now runs through the area. Note, in the lower photo, the cart of C & J Wiggins, Wash & Tar Contractors, from East Acton.

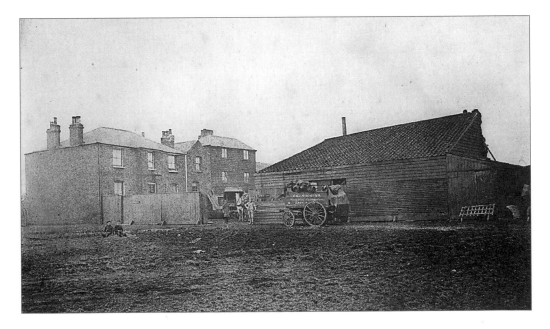

Neasden Stud Farm, *c.* 1880. A spectacular photograph with stunning clarity and definition. This view of the Stud Farm, Neasden Lane (opposite the Grange, *see* p. 39) is also the earliest local photograph featuring a member of the parish's black population. There is some debate as to the date of the photo and the gentleman remains unidentified. The Stud Farm was run by William Burton for many years between 1865 and 1920. He also owned the Kingsbury Polo Pony Stud Farm and had a contract for looking after Alfred Vanderbilt's polo ponies.

This is Dollis Hill Farm, *c.* 1890, which was rebuilt in about 1800. In 1664 a property on the site had been assessed under the Hearth Tax as having seven hearths, making it a considerable dwelling. In 1734 it was referred to as Dollis Hill House and in 1787 as Dollis Hill Farmhouse. In the writings of Harrison Ainsworth, the property features in the novel *Jack Sheppard* and the house is burgled by the highwayman Sheppard and his accomplice Blueskin. From the Post Office magazine of May 1939 we learn that: 'Dollis Hill Farm, the last farmhouse within five miles of Marble Arch, is to be demolished to make way for a new building.'

Sellon's Farm, *c.* 1875. This property was probably named after William Marmaduke Sellon who was in residence at 'Halsden Green' prior to 5 January 1825, when his will was proved. Indeed it was this gentleman who signed his name to an interesting protest against hunting which was drawn up 'At a Meeting of Nobleman, Farmers, and other Proprietors or Occupiers of Land in the Parishes of Harrow, Pinner, Watford, Stanmore, and their vicinities, held at Stanmore on the 15th day of June, 1808 . . . at which there was expressed great displeasure, not at hunting per se, but . . . that in this immediate district, so near to the Metropolis . . . the practice of hunting (under these peculiar circumstances) is attended with injuries too serious to be tolerated.'

Piles cowsheds, Waterloo Farm, Kilburn, 1880. This is another view which was used by Stanley Ball in his lecture, along with the view of the farmhouse that existed on the site until its demolition in 1855. Waterloo Farm was of particular interest to the early local officers as the site became the purpose-built council offices and town hall in Dyne Road (*see* p. 64). The cowsheds shown on this page were replaced by Dunster Gardens.

The Timbers, *c.* 1880, stood next to the White Hart in Church Road, where the Granada Cinema was later to be built. Some interesting information is available from the sales particulars of this property which was sold by auction in October 1875. 'Church Farm is most eligibly situate in Church End in the Parish of Willesden, and comprises an old-fashioned cottage residence called The Timbers. A tastefully arranged pleasure garden, well-shaded lawn with flower beds, two rustic summer houses, conservatory, and ornamental fish pond planted with white and yellow water lilies. Large well stocked and productive kitchen garden. Heated with hot water.'

Dudden Hill Farm, *c*. 1880. This photograph is described by F.A. Wood (pp. 35 and 62) as the 'House at the entrance to East's yard'. Dudden Hill Farm, some of the buildings of which are on the right of the picture, was run by a farmer called East towards the end of the nineteenth century and thus it became known as East's Farm or Yard. In a reminiscence from 1963, Stanley Miller says: 'A little way up Dudden Hill Lane stood an establishment where horses were broken in and trained. The building included a circular riding school which could not be seen properly as high walls enclosed the land on all sides, but the common sight was a pair of prancing horses harnessed to a vehicle consisting of nothing more than four wheels, their axles with a "tree" to connect them and a seat set up very high where the driver sat precariously perched controlling the steeds with varying degrees of success.'

Manor Farm in Harlesden, *c*. 1885. It stood a little to the north of where Manor Park Road and Park Parade now meet, and was demolished in about 1890. In February 1886 the estate was sold at auction. The tenant was Mr Banister whose daughter wrote some reminiscences in *Good Housekeeping* in 1949, describing how: 'Thomas Hughes proved the most generous of landlords, for during the great Cattle Plague of the 1878, when all our 200 cows had to be destroyed, he refused to accept any rent for that dreadful year. We children often played on the huge, grassy mounds that were the graves of our cattle.'

HOUSES

*Mon-Abri, the Shoot-up-Hill residence of Señor Manuel
Garcia. A celebrated teacher of singing, his pupils included
Jenny Lind. Born in Madrid on 17 March 1805 he died at
Mon-Abri on 1 July 1906, aged 101, having been decorated an
Honorary Commander of the Victorian Order.*

No. 52 Clifford Gardens, Kensal Rise, *c.* 1910. The building plan for this property, and indeed all the ten houses 50–68 Clifford Gardens, were approved on 23 June 1896, the property being completed on 8 December 1897 for Langler and Pinkham; the builder's address given as Mortimer Street, Kensal Rise. The first year that the property is listed in Kelly's Directory is 1899 when Mrs Studman was the occupier. In 1910, the suggested year of this photograph, the occupier was James Allum.

Pheasant Field Lodge, *c*. 1890. This property stood in Walm Lane between Willesden Green Station and Grosvener Road, according to Stanley Ball's notes. It was once the home of Revd William Huntington SS (1745–1813) who was a notorious and eccentric Calvanistic Methodist preacher. His explanation for the letters SS, which he used after his name, was 'As I cannot get a DD for want of cash, neither can I get a MA for want of learning, therefore I am compelled to fly for refuge to SS by which I mean Sinner Saved'.

Dr Whitby's house, Harlesden Terrace, *c*. 1880. Dr Robert Whitby MRCS, was at one time the only medical man resident in the parish of Willesden, according to reports in the local press. He came to Harlesden from Norfolk in about 1852, and he 'built up a capital practice in the early days of Harlesden's history, his clientele including almost the whole of the last generation of residents of repute'. In December 1894 the *Willesden Chronicle* carried an appeal to establish an annuity for Dr Whitby, which was signed by B.T. Atlay, Vicar of Willesden, and George Furness, among others. Dr Whitby died in October 1898, just a week after his wife, at the age of eighty.

Richmond Villa, Edgware Road, *c.* 1880. The property was near the Crown, Cricklewood, roughly where Oaklands Road meets Cricklewood Broadway. This fine house was owned by a Mrs Ann Metcalfe for many years: she was last listed in the Kelly's Directory in 1879. Living here in 1851 with her husband Thomas Metcalfe who was described as 'Superannuate Chelsea Hosp.'; by the time of the census enumerators returns in 1861 and 1871, she was widowed and was herself 'Annuitant'. She was clearly a woman of quite substantial independent means. Her household in 1871 consisted of William and Mary Eade, coachman and cook respectively, and Anne Smith, the housemaid. She was well-known locally for riding out in her horse and trap (*see* p. 49). In the lower photograph there is a possibility that the two women standing near the steps are the nieces listed in the 1871 returns, Hannah Barran and Ann Dixon.

These were the two Willesden residences of Frederick Augustus Wood from 1868 to 1894. Above is Brierley Villa and below is Hurworth. The latter is still in fine condition and is used as the West Willesden Conservative Club. Despite the large amount of time and effort that Wood expended on behalf of Willesden (whether in a public capacity or as the parish's historian) there is relatively little known of him personally. He and his wife came to the parish in about 1868 and in 1872 Mrs Wood is listed as a resident at Brierley Villa, although this clearly refers to his mother rather than his wife. Wood does not actually appear in the Kelly's Directory until 1880, just prior to the move from Brierley Villa to Hurworth, his mother having died in 1877. Indeed in 1882 there are two entries: 'Wood F.A. (Brierley Villa) Willesden Green' and 'Wood Frederick A. (Dunhallion tower) Stonebridge park W'. Among other things this shows there was a change of name for the latter property. Wood has left an impressive archive for which we can all be grateful; he was a particularly careful and thorough historian.

Cottage, High Road, Willesden, *c.* 1890. Henry Hobbs, the parish constable, lived in this house on High Road, Willesden Green. In the surviving parish papers of 1846 Hobbs is described as the policeman and at the time of the 1851 census, we learn that he was then thirty years old and was born in Rickmansworth, Hertfordshire. He was married to Hannah and had five children aged from five years to just ten months. In the 1871 census returns he was listed as a labourer, his wife was now Margaret and there were two children from the new marriage.

Church End House, *c.* 1910. This property, which is marked on the Ordnance Survey map of 1860, stood to the north of High Road, Willesden, between Neasden Lane and Brenthurst Road, and quite near to where the magistrate's court now stands. This photograph from the Wood Collection was probably taken in about 1890. At that time, a Mrs Rickards lived there and her building application no. 4703 requested permission to add a dairy farm and this was agreed to by the Urban District Council, on 19 April 1898.

The Grove, Neasden, *c.* 1915. A view of the back of the house (above), shows the tennis court and Master D.J. Glanfield with his fox terrier. This is the chauffeur (below) with the family car waiting outside the Grove in the period during the First World War (*see* p. 120). Note the AA badge at the centre of the windscreen. The main block of the house was built in the eighteenth century. Prior to being occupied by the Glanfields the residents were Edwin and Annie Tubbs, and their granddaughter Mrs M.D. Tanner remembered: 'It had a wonderful walled garden with peaches on the wall and a large walnut tree.'

Dollis Hill House, *c.* 1910. This house was built by the Finch family in 1825. They lived there until 1861. The house was then occupied by Lord Tweedmouth until 1881, and later his daughter and her husband, the Earl of Aberdeen, lived there until 1897. It was during the time of the Aberdeens that the property was visited by a number of important politicians, including Rosebery and Balfour. Its most famous visitor, however, was William Ewart Gladstone, after whom the park was named. Mark Twain (the author's real name was Samuel Clemens) stayed there briefly in 1900.

The Grange, Neasden, *c.* 1920. Originally a stable block for the Grove (*see* p. 37), it was converted in about 1720, when a new stable block was built, and became known as Rosetree Cottage. It was during this conversion that the building seems to have been given its Gothic windows. Items of particular interest are the remains of Neasden Green (*see* p. 43) in the foreground, with a chain-link fence around it, and the small one-story extension to the left of the building. The photo below shows the garden and the old conservatory of the Grange in about 1950.

Two interesting photos of the Grange undergoing restoration, in about 1975, prior to its opening as the London Borough of Brent's Museum of Community History. Above is the front of the building, after the removal of the porch which was to the left of the bay. The magnificent horse chestnut tree, to the right is now sadly gone. The main entrance to the museum is where the lower sash window was.

The interior of the Grange, gutted and laid bare. This is evidently the main staircase, prior to the elaborate reconstruction that was required. The property was finally saved after lying empty for many years. Elaborate schemes were drawn up as early as 1963, detailing how the Grange would exist on the roundabout in Neasden, together with a modern, purpose-built archive (around the area now occupied by the pond) and with pedestrian access over the roundabout to a new library in Neasden. While the council should be applauded for ensuring the survival of the building, accessibility remains a large problem.

The wellhouse at the Grange, *c.* 1965, in two unusual pictures which have previously remained unseen. This is before the house's restoration and conversion. As can be seen, the place was derelict and probably unworthy of retention. The photographs are important as a record of the museum building and its immediate environment before 1975. A visit to the Grange today will allow the visitor to see the surviving well in the attractive gardens.

Waterloo Cottage, Kilburn, *c.* 1875. This property, the site of which is now 207 Kilburn High Road, was located on the northern corner of where Willesden Lane meets the Kilburn High Road, with a frontage straight on to the main road. To the north of the house, on the 1865 Ordnance Survey map of the area, was a series of ten semi-detached villas which were known collectively as Waterloo. Further to the north, along the Kilburn Road, was the brewery and Waterloo Farm (*see* p. 29).

Dudden Hill Lane, 1922. This view is looking north-west towards Neasden Green (note the signpost and small white posts holding up the chain-link fence) with the Grange on the left near the second telegraph pole (*see* p. 39). This property was apparently known as Grove Lodge, but at the suggested date of the photograph had no separate entry in the Kelly's Directory, it was probably still an integral part of the estate of the Grove (*see* p. 37). Note also the two young girls standing next to telegraph pole in the centre of the picture.

The Grange, Willesden Green, *c.* 1875. Probably the house 'of rather superior description' which was built for Lord le Despenser and was later a part of William Weeden's estate. It was described as being on a knoll and commanding extensive views at the entrance to Chambers Lane. By 1873 it was up for sale as building land. It was bought by George Furness, but the land was not developed for building for some time, although the family's brickfields were established here (*see* p. 110). After 1873 the Grange was occupied by the managers of the Furness Estate, Mr J.W. Fry, Mr V. Goldsmith and Mr H.A. Burrell, before it was demolished in about June 1937.

Knowles Tower, *c.* 1890. This property occupied a site in what is now Longstone Avenue, opposite its junction with Drayton Road. It became part of George Furness's holding in about 1870. His son, George James, who was responsible for the development of the Cricklewood Park, Baker Farm (Harlesden) and Pleasant Row (Willesden Green) estates, lived there between 1898 and 1903. He followed the Thrupp family, Arthur Thrupp being listed as resident at Knowles Tower, Harlesden Lane, from 1877 to 1881 inclusive. Thereafter Mercy Thrupp was resident there until 1897. In describing the desire of the legal representatives of Mercy Thrupp to dispose of her property to the council, the *Willesden Chronicle* calls her ' . . . the eccentric hermit of Knowles Tower . . . '.

LANES

Dollis Hill Lane, c. 1930. On the extreme left of this photograph can be seen the gable of the Hermitage (116 Dollis Hill Lane) which is just beyond the two early Victorian cottages known as Dollis Hill or Scotch Cottages. In 1930 Fenn Kidson was resident at the Hermitage.

Cottage in High Road, Willesden, *c.* 1895. Demolished in 1897, the site is now 85–87 High Road. In 1901, when the new properties were first listed in the Kelly's Directories, Williams & Williams, Drapers were in business at 87 and 89 and in 1903 Henry Hart was running his fishmongers from the premises at 85 High Road.

Willesden High Road, *c.* 1905. This photograph was taken by an A. Anderson, who unfortunately is not listed in the local Kelly's Directories as his business was based in Harrow. On the rear of a postcard in the Cricklewood Archive can be found the following: 'A. Anderson Wholesale Pictorial Postcard Agent and local View Publisher, 107 West Street, Harrow on the Hill'. The horse and cart which can be seen in the middle distance (the younger passenger turning to look at the camera), belongs to the firm H. Dormer & Co., Kilburn, who were cheesemongers trading from 309 and 311 High Road, Kilburn until about 1909 when they last appeared in the Kelly's Directory.

Lower Oxgate Lane, *c.* 1920. The cottages in this photograph were built in the 1820s to house the cowmen of the old Oxgate Farm. The cottages were taken over by the War Office during the First World War. The original thatch was subsequently removed and replaced by tiles. The cottages were demolished in November 1937 to make room for the widening of Oxgate Lane.

Harlesden Lane, later Road, August 1895. A photograph taken at 2 p.m. on 24 August 1895. The wall of Roundwood House estate, home of George Furness, is on the left. Amos Beeson's history contains the following description: 'The lane along Mr Furness's garden was once so narrow that only a single vehicle could pass along. At this time [1870s] it was made wider, straightened, and the hedges planted. The old road turned the corner at the end of the garden path, went down the field and out again at what is now Roundwood Park.'

Acton Lane, *c.* 1900, seen in two intriguing, as well as attractive, photographs. It is evident, especially in the lower photograph, that there are men at work felling the trees. In between taking the two photos a crowd had gathered to watch the spectacle. In the background can be see the Baptist Church at Harlesden. This church was opened on 26 June 1890, '. . . with great rejoicing on the part of the Baptist denomination, and among many expressions of goodwill from sister communities . . . Briefly, it is handsome edifice – in fact it ranks as the finest of its kind in Harlesden.'

Dollis Hill Lane, *c.* 1890. The picture above is of Miss Metcalfe, who lived at Richmond Villa (*see* p. 34). Below are a number of cyclists pushing their bicycles down the rural lane. There is no recorded derivation of the name although the spelling, unsurprisingly, changed from Daleson (1593), through Dallyes and Dalleyes (1612 and 1619) to Dallis (1710), and finally, Dollis (1835). There is a suggestion that the name may be manorial or linked to a local family but neither derivation has been proved.

These cottages in Harlesden Road, *c*. 1880, were situated between James Wright's farm and Sellon's Farm (*see* p. 28), now Harlesden Gardens and Sellons Avenue. Amos Beeson related that 'James Wright was the owner of the next house and farm . . . There were three cottages on the farm land facing the road but set back. The last of these was used as a village school for about twenty boys and girls. This was run by an old schoolmaster named Griffiths and it was the best that could be had for young people at that time as there was no proper school then at hand.'

Mapes, or Willesden (Green) Lane, *c*. 1880. This was for many years known as Mapes Lane, after Walter Map, a well-known prelate who lived there in about 1140 to 1205 and who also gave his name to Mapesbury Manor. Interesting correspondence relating to the name of the lane being Maws appeared in the *Willesden Chronicle* in 1949, but there is a bequest contained in a will of 1554 which refers to the '. . . repair of Mapes Lane, which is between Kylborne and Wilsdon . . .'. The photograph (yet another from F.A. Wood's Collection) must date from about 1880. Note the elegant but widely spaced gaslights, the semi made-up state of the road, and the horse-drawn cart in the middle distance.

SECTION SEVEN

HOUSING

*1c and 1d Aylesbury Street, c. 1928. These concrete houses were built in 1927 by
the Metropolitan Railway Company for their employees. Threatened with demolition
in the late 1980s, they were granted conservation area status in October 1987.*

This is St Paul's Avenue, c. 1910, some years after the houses were constructed. Aside from the fact that this is a postcard view and therefore slightly easier to date, the plane trees that were presumably planted about the time of the street's completion are nearing maturity. Built on land acquired by compulsory purchase from the Dean and Chapter of St Paul's, the whole street was once called Chapter Road. The name changed to St Paul's Avenue in about 1907 – apparently for reasons of snobbery as this was the more expensive end of the street.

Hillside, Shoot-up-Hill, c. 1880. This impressive series of six mid-Victorian semi-detached houses were at Hillside, Shoot-up-Hill, Cricklewood. Note the elaborate driveway. They were built before the 1871 census when there were three families listed as resident at Hillside (although there were six houses; similarly in the 1872 Kelly's Directory, there are only two names). By far the most interesting occupant was William Richmond Mewburn who was described as the Secretary of the Union Bank of Australia.

Cottages in Grange Road in about 1890 (above) and 1929 (below). Two examples of James Thorne's '. . . mean brick cottages . . .' (see pp. 46, 47 and 50) as he described them in the 1876 *Handbook to the Environs of London*. They were still being cleared for new buildings as late as November 1958. The view above is from Stanley Ball's history lecture. These particular properties were in fact demolished in the 1930s. On 2 April 1939 the *Willesden Chronicle* commented. 'These cottages are said to be the oldest premises in Willesden. They were occupied until three weeks ago when the last tenants left . . . Once these cottages faced the village green.'

No. 46 Nicoll Road, Harlesden, *c.* 1920. This property is first listed in the Kelly's Directory for 1884, when Josh. Shubrook was resident and the house was known as Hamilton Villa. In March 1893 Mr Shubrook made an application to the Willesden Local Board for a conservatory to be added to the property. This was duly approved with the builders, Tennant & Co of Willesden Green, commencing works on 9 March. The fees payable were 4*s* 6*d*.

No. 2 Nicoll Road, Harlesden, April 1935. This house stood at the junction of Nicoll Road and Acton Lane, and it is seen here in the process of demolition. Dr Rawes was resident at the property from 1921 (when he is listed as Chas. Kinsman Rawes) until 1935 (when he is Chas. K. Rawes, MB, Physician and Surgeon). The property was also called The Elms and this was the name given to the twenty-four flats that were built in its place.

West Ella Road, *c.* 1928. The young plane trees that lined the road reached maturity, but were cut down in 1979 after being blamed for subsidence. The road took its name from West Ella Cottage which existed on the site until about 1897. Note the ironwork on the front garden walls which was removed during the Second World War to help with the war effort.

No. 39 Larch Road, in 1897. This was part of the Cricklewood Park Estate laid out by George Furness and his son, George James. The shop on Cricklewood Broadway (*see* p. 95) appears to have been part of this development. George Furness was responsible for comparatively few houses in Willesden, despite indications to the contrary. However, towards the end of his life, he was deeply involved in the purchase and laying out of the streets and sewers, and the construction of houses on the Cricklewood Park Estate.

Priory Park Road in 1947 (above) and Christchurch Avenue, *c*. 1950 (below). Two of the very few post-1945 pictures to be found in the Cricklewood Archive. The picture of Priory Park Road shows war damage being repaired and two workmen can be clearly seen on the scaffolding. Note the massive timber prop, partially hidden by the scaffolding. Below is a view of 94, 96 and 98 Christchurch Avenue taken from the garden of no. 77, known as Rose Dene from 1904 until 1923 when it was occupied by Ellis Thomas Powell, and latterly, his widow. When this site was redeveloped in the 1960s the name was restored and the flats are known collectively as Rosedene.

The canal feeder, c. 1925. Another view of the canal feeder can be seen on page 9, although this was taken some forty years later. However, the principal activity in the photograph is the same as in the previous one, despite the intervening years. That is, of course, fishing for tiddlers. Behind the three figures can be seen the rear of houses in Bridge Road. To the left, beyond the railway embankment, are the backs of the terraced houses in Berry Street. Incredible as it seems, the small footbridge seen here is shown on the Ordnance Survey map.

The Brentwater Estate, c. 1930. An aerial view showing the open expanse of water known as the Welsh Harp. In the foreground is the controlled Willesden Borough Council building scheme which planned to ensure that new housing avoided the problems of overcrowding so evident in Kilburn and parts of Harlesden. Some 100 council houses, mostly on this estate, had been built by the end of 1933. Another large council estate was built at Curzon Crescent in 1936.

Reconstructed war-damaged houses on Aboyne Road, *c.* 1947. The road runs up to the North Circular Road, at the junction of which is Neasden Library (*see* p. 68). The road was named after the Aberdeenshire village where the previous owner, Colonel Randall James Nichol, had his home. The street was bombed twice in the war; first in 1941 when a solitary bomb dropped there which caused no deaths, but some properties had to be demolished. On 15 March 1945, however, the road was the victim of a V2 rocket. Roofs were blown up, houses collapsed, eight people died and forty were injured.

Bramshill Road, Harlesden, at its junction with Harley Road, *c.* 1920. Bramshill Lodge stood to the west of the junction of Acton Lane and Station Road. The retaining wall is that of the North London Line between Harlesden and Willesden Junction. The flooding remains a mystery.

WILLESDEN FACES

*'Some of the family at Neasden', c. 1927. This picture
from an unprovenanced family album is an ideal example
of the type of material that continues to be deposited with
the Cricklewood Archive but which cannot be effectively
catalogued due to the lack of information available.*

The butcher, the baker, the candlestick maker. Well, not quite, but a vivid view of the Crown Inn, Harlesden, in 1877. This is an exciting photograph for a number of reasons; the image has good provenance, and there are a number of copies of it in the collections of the Cricklewood Archive, but more importantly, we know the names of a number of people in this picture. From the left is Thomas Wills, the butcher, holding two knives; Mr Haylor, who was for many years the rate collector (*see* p. 62); Mr G. Price, the grocer, and his boy; Mr Haskins, Mr Johnson and Mr W. Lane (holding the horse's reins). The date of this photo is known because of a notice in the bay window of the pub concerning the sale of freehold building land on Friday, 22 June 1877.

The Revd J.C. Wharton, with his wife and their son Charles, outside Willesden Vicarage. Wharton was vicar from 1864 until 1888 when he was succeeded by Revd B.T. Atlay, MA. There is some uncertainty concerning the vicar's retirement. An anonymous letter in the Wood collection refers to Wharton's 'dreadful affliction' and the letter actually suggests setting up a Testimonial Fund to pay off the vicar's debts. However, there is no indication of whether or not this was acted upon nor how the vicar came to be in debt.

Willesden Methodist Church Hall, 1914. This rare view of some of the early black population in Willesden comes from the visual archive of the Welsh Methodist or Presbyterian Church of Wales, Willesden Lane. The movement to establish the church began in April 1898 when the Willesden Green Assembly Rooms were obtained for temporary use for morning and evening services. A chapel registered for religious service by the Welsh Calvinistic Methodists was opened in Willesden Lane in 1900. This was replaced in 1911 by the church still existing today.

Children fishing in the River Brent, c. 1920. This picture is taken from a collection of excellent photographs that were loaned to the Cricklewood Archive in 1985. They were all taken by Frank Pitcher of Quainton or Verney Street in Neasden. Mr Pitcher's grandson brought the images to the archives for copying and took some reprints away for further identification, although it seems that this course of action did not result in any further information about the content of the photographs coming to light.

Willesden Board of Guardians, *c.* 1900. An informal portrait of Jimmy Perkins (left), a Willesden Guardian of the Poor, enjoying the warmth of the fire with the Master of the Hendon Union workhouse. Perkins (*see* p. 10) became Chair of the Guardians in April 1906, his colleague Mr Chamberlain congratulated him as '. . . he was one of the oldest members of the Board, and he felt sure Mr Perkins would make a very good chairman'. He was a Guardian from 1897 until his sudden death at his home in Fortune Gate Road, Harlesden in 1913. He was also closely connected with the Harlesden Baptist Church (*see* p. 48).

Willesden Local Board, June 1887. A photograph taken in the gardens of the Spotted Dog at Neasden, where the Local Board held their annual dinner. Among the group are a number of well-known local names. Mr F.A. Wood, who was Chair of the Board when this photograph was taken, is seated at the centre. To the left is Oscar Claude Robson, the Surveyor and to the right Samuel Tilley, Clerk to the Board. At the back, on the extreme right is Mr Haylor, the Collector, while third from the right is Stanley Ball, Second Clerk.

LOCAL GOVERNMENT

Stanley Ball, c. 1895. Ball was employed by the Willesden local authorities for over forty-six years before his death at the age of sixty-seven. Serving initially as Deputy Clerk he was appointed Clerk to the Willesden Urban District Council in 1896. One of Willesden's keenest local historians, his lantern-slide lecture has provided a number of the views reproduced here.

Willesden Town Hall, Dyne Road, 1930. When the Willesden Local Board was established in 1875, their first home was the North London Hotel. Subsequently, the officers moved to Hampton House, now 297 High Road, Kilburn. By 1886 it was abundantly clear that the offices at Hampton House were too small and cramped for the increasing amount of work the local authority were expected to undertake. Land was purchased at Waterloo Farm (*see* p. 29) and an architectural competition held, Mr Harnor's design finally being accepted in January 1887. The total cost of the construction and furnishing of the building was £10,204 12*s* 1*d* and the members and staff of the Willesden Local Board moved there in November 1891. The photo below shows the boardroom at Dyne Road in 1924.

On 10 August 1933 George V signed the warrant which declared 'The . . . said district comprised within the limits set forth . . . is hereby created a Municipal Borough by the name of "Borough of Willesden" '. In this photograph can be seen (from the right): The Charter Mayor, Councillor George H. Hiscocks, receiving the Charter from the Lord Mayor of London, Sir Percy Greenaway; in between them is the Charter Clerk, Mr E.A. Pratt. To the extreme left, at the top of the picture is Dr J.S. Crone (*see* p. 81): at this time he was High Sheriff of Middlesex. The gentleman who is level with Dr Crone is Major A.E. Wood, the Sword Bearer, while just below them is Councillor Leigh-Mossley, Deputy Charter Mayor and Chair of the Council.

Willesden Charter of Incorporation, Thursday, 7 September 1933. Here the dignitaries are seated on the podium, while the Charter Mayor gives his speech. Note the gentlemen of the press huddled to the left of the picture and the guard of honour. The actual Charter ceremony took place at King Edward VII recreation ground (*see* pp. 85 and 86), where there was a choir of some 2,000 schoolchildren and the trumpeters of the Life Guards sounded a fanfare during the presentation.

Charter Day Luncheon, Tuesday 5 September 1933. A complimentary luncheon was laid on by the Rotary Clubs of Willesden East and West at the White Hart Hotel to which the members of the Willesden Council, the Willesden members of the Middlesex County Council, Justices of the Peace and council officials were invited. Following the lunch the national anthem was sung and then Mr G.F. Mallard, President of Willesden East Rotary Club, welcomed the guests and remarked that the Rotarians of Willesden were met to pay honour to their civic leaders on the occasion of the Incorporation of Willesden.

LIBRARIES

*Kilburn Library, in Salusbury Road, was the first branch library to be opened in Willesden. Revd J.E.C.
Welldon, headmaster of Harrow School, performed the official ceremony on 30 January 1894 when the
library's initial book stock amounted to 3,957 volumes.*

In 1891 the Willesden Local Board adopted the Free Libraries Act. Three libraries were then opened in 1894; Kilburn (*see* p. 67), Willesden Green (*see* p. 69) and Harlesden in Craven Park Road. This is a drawing of the Harlesden Library by the architect John Cash, of 55 Buckingham Road, Harlesden. When opened by Sir Henry Roscoe, MP, on 14 February 1894, the library was only a small part of the current building, with a book stock of just 6,411 volumes. The opening brochure from which this drawing is taken relates to the opening of the large reading room which was added to the rear in June 1903. Further additions came in 1910, and in 1930 Harlesden was the last Willesden library to be converted to public access.

Neasden Library, opened at the junction between Aboyne Road (*see* p. 58) and the North Circular Road on 28 February 1931. The architect commented: 'Advantage has been taken of the peculiar shape of the site to plan the building on entirely novel lines. The main entrance is place on the angle, and is flanked on the North Circular road frontage by the Reading Room, and on the Aboyne Road frontage by the Children's Room. In the summer the flat roof over the Lending Library will be utilized as an Open-air Reading Room (above), commanding a very pleasant view over the Recreation Ground and the extensive stretch of water known as the "Welsh Harp".

Willesden Green Library, *c.* 1900, was opened by Mr Irwin E.B. Cox, MP, for the Harrow Division on 18 July 1894, with a book stock of 4,968 volumes. The proposed adoption of the Public Libraries Act elicited a good deal of discussion within the columns of the local press, as on the eve of the vote, 20 February 1891: 'There is just time for a few last words on the Public Library Question, for although the voting papers were delivered at every house in Willesden yesterday, we cannot suppose they have been more than unfolded yet . . . The arguments for and against are two in number — no more. A Public Library will be a great factor for good; it must help to raise up an intelligent and educated people to whom England's honour can be safely trusted. On the other hand every householder will have an extra charge imposed upon him, say from 1*s* 6*d* upwards according to circumstances.' The vote resulted in a majority of 1,187 in favour of its adoption.

Kensal Rise, *c.* 1906. As soon as 1896 there was agitation in favour of a library for Kensal Rise and land was donated for the purpose by the Warden and Fellows of All Souls College, Oxford. However, it proved difficult to find the money necessary to build the new library. It was then agreed that £100 and one-tenth of the penny rate would be used for the provision of a reading room only. This was duly opened by Samuel Clemens (Mark Twain) on 27 September 1900. Soon a small lending department was begun, with just 1,100 volumes, in the lobby of the reading room. Thereafter an application was made to Dr Andrew Carnegie for financial assistance, in September 1903. Carnegie agreed to provide a sum not exceeding £3,000 for the extensions. The newly-extended library was opened on 13 May 1904.

Cricklewood Library, 1929. Cricklewood was one of the last Willesden libraries to open. The Rt. Hon. Lord Riddell performed the official opening ceremony at 3.00 p.m. on 8 June 1929 when, as can be seen to the right of this picture, some areas of the district remained free from development. The building has changed little, although the 1960s 'improvements' in moving the main entrance to the front now appear misguided. The photograph below shows the refreshments available to the dignitaries after the official opening. The library building now also houses the London Borough of Brent's archive service.

HOSPITALS

The Micklethwaite family, Willesden Institution, c. 1914. Ben Micklethwaite is seen here with his wife and daughter. A pre-First World War visit to the Workhouse Infirmary would require the visitor to ring the bell which would be answered by Mr Micklethwaite. Among his other duties he was also expected to report nurses who returned to the institution late.

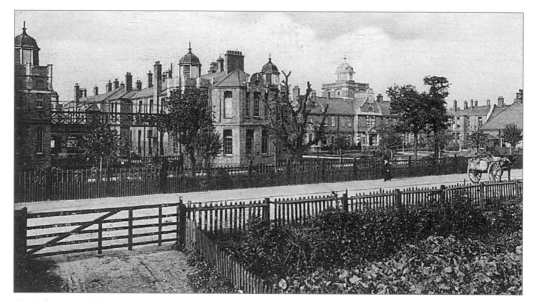

The Infirmary, Willesden, *c.* 1905. Willesden withdrew from the Hendon Poor Law Union in 1896 and for a few years a private house was used as an infirmary. In 1897 a 60-acre site was acquired (at a cost of £14,000) in Acton Lane, the designs of Alfred Saxon Snell, FRIBA, being accepted for the construction of the buildings. Initial impressions of Willesden Workhouse Infirmary (there was accommodation for 400 people, including 150 sick) were not good: 'Our . . . representative . . . found . . . everywhere deplorable overcrowding. In the able-bodied men's ward the beds were jammed so closely together that there was not room to stand between them', noted the *Municipal Journal* in March 1903.

Central Middlesex County Hospital, 1945. A photograph which may show the aftermath of a V2 attack which occurred at 2.30 a.m. on Sunday 28 January. This resulted in no serious injuries although one building was demolished. There is some doubt, however, as to whether this is actually Central Middlesex Hospital, as is often the case with photographs dating from wartime the original caption did not mention the locality and this has been subsequently supplied at a later date.

Willesden Municipal Hospital, *c.* 1920. This is the isolation hospital built by the Urban District Council in 1904 on a 10-acre site in Dog Lane (now Brentfield Road). Despite being extended in 1904 and changing its name to Willesden Municipal Hospital during the First World War, strong arguments that it should become a general hospital went unheeded, and it reverted to being a fever hospital offering 138 beds in 1922. Although it was again extended in the 1930s and a block for the treatment of eye disease was added in 1950, by 1975 the number of beds in use had fallen to 175, from a high point of 200. In 1970 it was in use as a geriatric hospital, and in 1987 the hospital was closed and demolished. Below is an internal view of one of the laboratories at the hospital, probably in the 1930s.

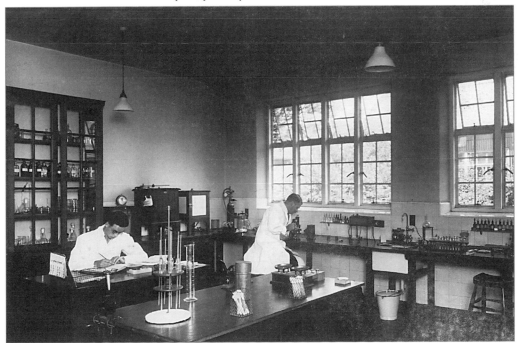

Willesden Municipal Hospital, *c*. 1930. In this other view of Willesden Municipal Hospital, there is some evidence that this photograph and the one on the previous page are contemporaneous. Mitchell (or Slade) Brook, a tributary of the River Brent (*see* pp. 1, 4, 7 and 8) ran through the grounds.

Willesden Cottage Hospital, *c*. 1910. The formal opening of the building opening took place on 18 July 1893 when Miss Balfour (her father the Rt. Hon. Arthur J. Balfour accompanying her) performed the ceremonial duties. The hospital was built after a gift from the well-known philanthropist Passmore Edwards, indeed he also supplemented local fund-raising in order to extend the hospital in 1899, when it became known as The Passmore Edwards Hospital for Willesden. The name was changed to Willesden General Hospital after further extensions in 1921.

FIRE SERVICES

*'Captain Mitchell, Willesden's first Fireman', in about
1880, according to Stanley Ball. In actual fact Mitchell
was superintendent of the Kilburn Fire Brigade, having
succeeded his father. He died suddenly at the age of thirty-
seven, leaving a wife and three children.*

Willesden firefighters, *c.* 1875. Another fine image from the lantern slide collection of Stanley Ball (p. 63). Unfortunately this one does not have the same degree of description as some of the other images reproduced herein. It is interesting to note that this formal portrait also includes a picture of a member of the police force. When the Volunteer Fire Brigade was formally wound up in 1932, the Chair of the Urban District Council commented in the *Willesden Chronicle*: 'Never in the history of Willesden . . . had such wonderful voluntary service been tendered as by their Fire Brigade, and they were all very proud indeed of them. He hoped that all the men who were being disbanded now would be ready to help and co-operate with the professional firemen should occasion arise, and, in any case, when they heard the clanging of the fire bell, they would have the satisfaction of knowing that "the other blokes" were doing the job.'

This photograph, taken after 1873 when a fire led to the addition of a more modern wing to the building, shows the White Horse (*see* p. 20) and the second Willesden fire engine. The shed where the engine was housed can be seen to the right, it was moved here from the churchyard because it was difficult to remove it from the churchyard quickly. This engine was purchased second-hand from the manufacturers Shand and Mason by public subscriptions at a cost of £90. Mr Morley, the captain, is seated on the box with the reins in his hand, Walter Douse is holding the horses' heads and Kendall jnr, son of an earlier Willesden firefighter, is standing on the engine.

The Willesden Volunteer fire brigade, which was founded at Church End in 1872 and not officially disbanded until 1932. The main station was the White Horse, Church End, until the late 1880s when it moved to the vestry hall in Neasden Lane. The parish vestry first appointed a salaried keeper of the fire engine in 1840, the office continuing until 1884. However, it was the fire which destroyed the mill on Shoot-up-Hill (*see* p.109) that exposed the inefficiency of the existing services. In the aftermath the Kilburn, Willesden and St John's volunteer fire brigade was established in 1863. By 1872 the brigade covered the eastern part of the parish from its headquarters in Bridge Street, Kilburn, until the Local Board took control of the fire services in the early 1890s.

'A Fireman's Funeral' from the *Willesden Chronicle* on 5 February 1892. 'A well-known member of the local fire brigade in the person of Mr Robert Watts, of 8, Greenhill Park, Harlesden, has been removed from our midst, primarily through an attack of influenza . . . which resulted in his death on Thursday, the 28th ult., at the early age of 32. The funeral took place at Willesden Cemetery on Tuesday, the remains being laid to rest with full honours. Shortly before 1 o'clock the Kilburn detachment of the Local Board Fire Brigade arrived with the steamer at the headquarters of their Harlesden brethren, over which the national flag was floating at half-mast . . . . Up to this point the weather had been fine, though cold and threatening, but as the procession passed down Church Road a drizzling rain began to fall, and when at the entrance to the cemetery the coffin was lifted off the bier on to the shoulders of six firemen, hail and rain descended in torrents, drenching to the skin all who had had the temerity to face the elements without an umbrella or overcoat. . . During the whole time occupied in reading the service inside the hall, a heavy rain was falling, and this continued while the service at the graveside was being performed and till long after the relatives had left the church-yard, when after a heavy snowstorm the air suddenly cleared and the weather became as bright as had been the case earlier in the day.'

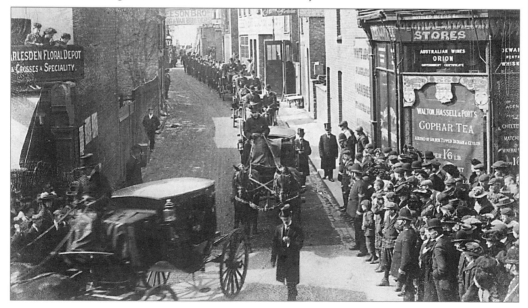

RECREATION

A view of the playground in Gladstone Park, c. 1910, with
children playing with the swings (see p. 80).

In 1900, with financial help from Middlesex County Council and despite strong objections from some ratepayers, Willesden Urban District Council bought most of the Dollis Hill Estate from the Finch family. The 96 acres were left as the parkland and gardens of a country house while 29 acres on the southern side of the railway line were made into sports pitches. The park was named after one of its famous visitors – William Ewart Gladstone. The house itself was bought in 1908 and opened a year later as refreshment rooms. Here can be seen the children's play area (above) and the kidney-shaped open-air swimming pool (below).

A photograph of the participants in the Hospital Carnival at Shootbred's Ground, c. 1900. Luckily the names of many of the people in the photograph are known, especially the centre couple who are Mr and Mrs George J. Furness, of Roundwood House (previously of Knowles Tower, *see* p. 44). To the left of the picture is Charles Biddiscombe and his wife and between the two couples is Surgeon Major Eames, RN; his wife is seated to the right of Mrs Furness (née Eames).

Dr Crone's garden party in Roundwood Park, 1900. It is impossible to say what the purpose of this social occasion was, although Crone was one of the many active members of the Willesden political and social establishment that left a visual archive (*see* p. 65). In his later years the *Chronicle* had this to say about him: 'Willesden's Literary Doctor and genial Magistrate, Dr J.S. Crone, was for three successive years Chairman of the Willesden District Council. One of the pioneers of public libraries in Willesden, he served on the Central Libraries Committee . . . . An Ulsterman, he is Editor of the "Irish Booklover", he is an enthusiastic book collector, and he was once Consulting Editor and a regular contributor to this journal.'

Roundwood Park, *c.* 1920. Roundwood Park was opened by Sir R.M. Littler, KC (Chairman of the Middlesex County Council) on 11 May 1895 after having been bought and laid out by the Willesden Local Board at the cost of £25,956. In the *Official Guide to Willesden, 1923–24* the park is described as: '. . . a delightful public resort. From a steep hill . . . some delightful views are to be obtained. Looking westward one sees Harrow-on-the-Hill, and the new Wembley Stadium. To the south one sees Roundwood House [the residence of Mr G.J. Furness, MP (*see* p. 81) for the West Division of Willesden], pleasantly embowered in trees.'

A view of Neasden golf course which existed from 1893 until the 1930s building boom swamped the area. The club house was Neasden House, which was first called this by Sir William Roberts who, in about 1650, demolished medieval cottages adjacent and concentrated the area into gardens and orchards around the house. It was the building of the North Circular road and the widening of Neasden Lane for the British Empire Exhibition that led to the biggest wave of building in Neasden. By 1929, building was in progress on the links and the area was covered by semi-detached houses in 1937. Neasden House succumbed to the building boom and in 1933 Neasden Court, Cairnfield Avenue, was built on the site.

Queen's Park was opened in 1887 on land formerly used for the Royal Agricultural Show. Public meetings held during 1883 led to the presentation of a petition to the Corporation of London which requested the purchase of the show ground for the population of Kilburn. It was the Church Commissioners who owned the 30-acre site and they duly presented it to the Corporation, who opened Queen's Park in 1887, in honour of the Queen's Jubilee.

'Queen's Park Tree Struck by Lightning. On the occasion of the single purely local thunderclap and flash of lightning, on Saturday night, one of the poplar trees in Queen's Park was struck. Part of the tree was cut to the ground, and the white, barked section of the trunk, remained gauntly staring. The original height of the tree was about 50 feet; the remaining portion is only 30 feet in height. A large bough, at least a foot in thickness, was wrenched away by the shock. A large number of the leaves among the foliage lying on the ground after the flash were scorched black by the effect of the lightning. On Sunday there was quite a "pilgrimage" to Queen's Park, of people living in the vicinity. Many children seized pieces of splintered wood and bore them away as souvenirs.' (*Willesden Chronicle*)

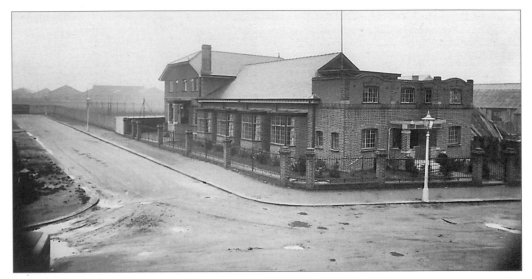

Harold Wesley Limited's Community Hall, Harlesden, *c.* 1930. The company was formed in 1905 when they were based in Worship Street in the City of London and the business moved to Acton Lane in 1925. In 1965 one of the company's boasts was that: 'We make the cheapest toilet rolls in the country'. As well as building the community hall the company built houses for its employees at Harold Road and Wesley Avenue. A perusal of the 1935 Ordnance Survey map shows that the building above was called the Wesley Social Hall and that Wesley playing fields were a short distance from the factory at the end of Harold Road and Wesley Avenue.

Constitutional Club, St Mary's Road, Harlesden, *c.* 1910. The plans for the club were submitted to the Local Board on 20 February 1893, the applicant being Mr F. Shaw. However, the initial plans were disapproved on 28 February before re-admission but they were approved on 14 March. The club had a chequered history, becoming Harlesden Labour Bureau in 1914, when the *Chronicle* said: 'It is the irony of fate that a Conservative Hall, after passing through so many vicissitudes, should at length be acquired by a Radical Government, for the purposes of a scheme which it is generally admitted is one of the greatest failures that that even a Radical Government has conferred upon us.'

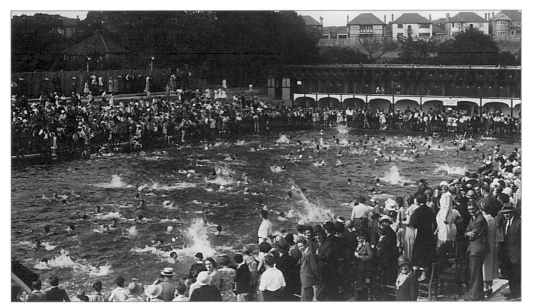

The swimming baths at King Edward VII Park, Willesden, *c.* 1930. The park was renamed Willesden Sports Centre in 1965 to avoid confusion with King Edward VII Park in Wembley. Here the pool is being used for competitive swimming. The park, a little over 27 acres, was acquired by the then District Council in November 1909. Interestingly in the *Official Guide to Willesden 1923-24* the following can be read: 'Here, as in Gladstone Park (*see* pp. 79 and 80), there is an . . . open-air swimming bath . . . . It differs in that it is from 6 feet 3 inches to 3 feet 3 inches, and there is no diving platform. But there is a third dissimilarity to be noted, perhaps, from the bathers' point of view, the most important of all. In this bath mixed bathing – which is becoming more popular and more general, and when conducted under proper conditions, more to be advocated . . . is permitted during certain times . . . .'

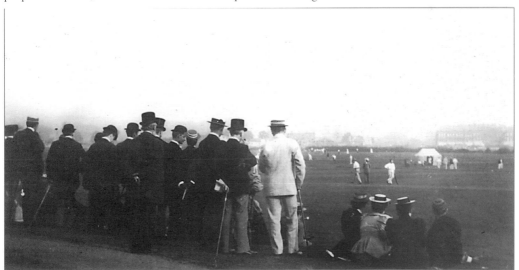

The cricket field at Walm Lane, *c.* 1890, from a picture in Stanley Bell's lecture. The precise location of this cannot be pinpointed on the Ordnance Survey maps. The Black Lion Perseverance Club was playing matches as early as 1854, the ground described as being '. . . on the Willesden side of Kilburn'. Willesden cricket club was in existence by 1875 but its ground, which was at Church End until 1898, could not be the one shown here.

Allotments, Harlesden, *c.* 1947. There were also allotments at King Edward VII Recreation Ground (*see* p. 85). Allotments continued to provide a source of additional food supplies in the aftermath of war, but in a survey in May 1966 of allotment provision, it was declared that: 'Following the end of the last war, during which many open spaces had been dug up as allotments [the total area of allotments in Wembley and Willesden then amounted to more than 500 acres and nearly 7,000 plots], there was a rapid decrease in the number of allotments in Brent as temporary wartime sites were restored to their former use.'

A street merry-go-round in Minet Avenue, *c.* 1930, full of children enjoying the ride. The merry-go-round sits on a horse-drawn cart while the gentleman shown here works the machinery with the handle visible in the photograph. A donation from a former resident of the road, Mr R.E.B. Welham, it can only be surmised whether he was one of the children in the picture.

TRANSPORT

The old station house at the junction of the West London Railway and the London and Birmingham was built in 1844, to allow passengers to interchange. Unfortunately it did not provide access for local residents; they still had to use the old Willesden station at Acton Lane. It had a very short operational life (10 June to 30 November 1844) but was not demolished until the 1950s.

Willesden Green Station, *c.* 1925. The first Metropolitan Line station opened here on 24 November 1879. From 1894 to 1938 it was known as Willesden Green & Cricklewood. The rebuilt station illustrated here was designed by C.W. Clarke. The diamond-shaped clock was a trademark of his style.

Kendall Road and Gladstone Park, *c.* 1910. A large, happy group out for an evening stroll through Gladstone Park. They are negotiating the level crossing of the Midland and South Western Junction railway, from the park to the west end of Kendal Road. The level crossing was replaced with a footbridge which is still in everyday use.

Brondesbury Station from the platform, c. 1906 (above) and from the junction between Shoot-up-Hill and Iverson Road, c. 1910 (below). Brondesbury station was opened on 2 January 1860 as Edgware Road station, being renamed Brondesbury in 1873. The train seen pulling into the station in the upper picture is en route for Kew Bridge station on the London and North Western and North London railway. This picture is dated 1906 and the photographer was A. Anderson of 107 West Street, Harrow on the Hill (p. 46).

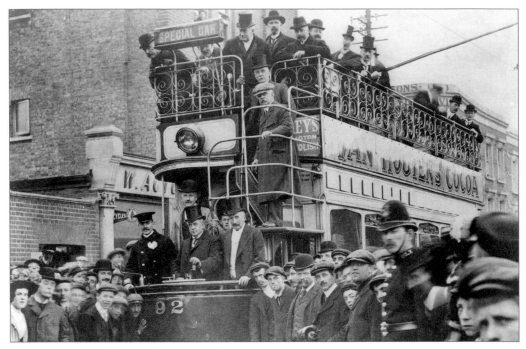

'First Tramcar to Willesden, 7 October 1909.' A formal portrait of the dignitaries in a tramcar on route 92 with a large and interested crowd in the street. The local newspaper gave the event little space but did say 'New Tram Line Opened. The tramway extension of the Middlesex County Council linking up Willesden Junction and Acton by Victoria Road was opened yesterday by Mr Herbert Neild, MP, who drove the first car, whilst the return car was driven by County Alderman Chas. Pinkham, JP, CC. The ceremony was attended by Dr J.S. Crone, JP, CC, Mr E. Metcalfe, CC, Councillor W.R. Dunn, Mr S.W. Ball, Mr H.T. Wakelam, etc.'

Cricklewood Broadway, *c.* 1910. A Metropolitan Electric Tramways tramcar no. 105 (type A), preparing to leave the Cricklewood terminus spur at Ash Grove, calling at Hendon and Edgware. This is the Barnet side of the Broadway, nos 102–120, right to left, with Arthur Whitney's tobacconist's shop on the left. A number of tramway schemes were planned from the Crown going down the Edgware Road, but due partly to the opposition of the London County Council, Hampstead Metropolitan Borough Council and Willesden Urban District Council, the Light Railway Commissioners refused to sanction any of the plans.

The Grand Junction Canal, *c.* 1910. The heavily loaded narrow boat has illegally moored in the bridge hole, presumably while the boatmen had a pint in the Grand Junction Arms. Possibly the official moorings needed dredging and could not accommodate a boat loaded to the gunnels (*see* p. 10).

The Crown Hotel, Cricklewood, *c.* 1910. An impressive collection of horse buses are seen here at their terminus. In the middle of the photograph is a single motor omnibus while to the right is the delivery cart of W. Melhish, Flour Factor of Camberwell. Note the impressive architecture of the Hulls' store to the left, and above the buses (*see* p. 96).

A steam engine accident at Neasden, during the General Strike, 1926. The Cricklewood Archive contains a number of photographs of Neasden depot and local incidents that occurred during the strike. The story behind this picture is this: 'The next memory that comes flooding in was the great day when the first steam engine at Neasden was lit and steamed up. As the steamer came out of the sheds, all the volunteer signalmen at the signal box leant out of the windows and cheered at the effort of getting the steamer going and the steamer made towards the express rails, but in their excitement the volunteer signalmen had forgotton to set the points for the engine and it simply turned over on its side blocking the whole of both express lines. It took volunteers and cranes four days to get the steamer off the lines and repair the rails.'

A view of Neasden Station taken from Dog Lane Bridge (now the North Circular Road), c. 1930. This station, on the Metropolitan Line which was extended to Aylesbury in 1892, was opened in 1880. For fifty years the station was known as Kingsbury and Neasden station, until it changed in 1932. The Metropolitan built a power station next to the workshops at Neasden in 1903 and electric trains, first run in 1905, began to supersede steam. In 1979 this section of track became part of the Jubilee Line.

Neasden Lane from Jackman's Corner, R101 passing over, 1929. This photograph was probably taken by the owner of the forge in Neasden (*see* p. 113), Mr Henry George Jackman, whose obituary in the *Willesden Chronicle* in 1962 calls him the 'Last Village Blacksmith'. The forge closed in 1930 and Mr Jackman eventually left London for retirement in Eastbourne.

General Strike, Neasden, 1926. A volunteer signalman at Neasden Box, sustained by half a light ale and twenty Players, was perhaps one of the unfortunate souls who had the responsibility of de-railing a locomotive during the strike (*see* p. 92). One local resident who was a volunteer driver during the strike was very clear as to his feelings: ' I was a young man and I thoroughly enjoyed the volunteer work in the strike, and was very sorry when the strike was over as I had had so many really interesting adventures, including going down to the Neasden works and helping repair the trains that had broken down.'

Two pictures of the Willesden Heliport, probably at the Welsh Harp. These were both donated to the Cricklewood Archive by Mr A.G. Beckett (Director of Development) in February 1978. They had been given to him by Councillor Henry Berney who had asked that they be passed on to the archive. Sadly little other information is given but the fact is that the prints '. . . relate to an episode in Willesden Council's postwar life when they, along with many other local authorities in Britain, were very concerned to ensure adequate provision was made in their particular Boroughs for helicopter landing places.'

SHOPS

Walter James Cartwright's grocers shop on Cricklewood Broadway, c. 1900. This attractive image comes from the George Furness archive and the shop may have been built by Furness himself, although this remains unproven. The property survives, on the corner of Ashford Road and the Broadway.

Cricklewood Broadway, *c.* 1910. This picture can be found in the Kelly's Directory of 1910 and must therefore date from around that time. It gives a good impression of the way the Broadway was developed and helps to put the photographs of the Crown (*see* p. 91) and W.B. Hulls' store (below and p. 91) in perspective. This photograph is taken from around the junction of the Broadway and Ash Grove, on the left, looking towards Shoot-up-Hill.

W.B. Hulls' impressive store on Cricklewood Broadway, *c.* 1905. Next door to the Crown (p. 91) and thus not actually in the parish of Willesden, it is inconceivable that locals would not have used the store on a regular basis. The lively Edwardian architecture survives in part although the fine bay and balcony, seen at the left of the store (beyond which is Cricklewood Lane), has unfortunately been lost. Thankfully its original twin (*see* p. 91) which is out of this picture, has survived.

A photograph of George Waller's window display, *c.* 1905. Waller's shops were at 54–56 High Road, Willesden. The business is listed in the *Kelly's Kilburn, Willesden, Harlesden, & c., Directory* ('Buff Book') for the years 1897 to 1907 inclusive, where it is described as George Waller, tailor, boot and shoe maker. In 1908 the premises were occupied by City Tailoring Co. (54 High Road), C.R. Dargel, hairdresser and Frederick Gale, bootmaker (56 High Road).

Manze's Pie and Eel shop, 147 Canterbury
Road, *c.* 1930. These premises first appear in
the Kelly's Directory in 1926 when the name of
the shop is mistakenly given as Mange's. This
was corrected in the 1927 edition and the entry
remained unchanged until the last edition of the
Kelly's Directory for Willesden was published
in 1940. The business was still in existence in
1963 when the shop front looked remarkably
unchanged.

Harlesden High Street, *c.* 1910. a tobacconists and
confectioners shop near to the Jubilee Clock, the
shopkeeper at the time being 'Miss Shaw,
confectioner' and it could well be her standing in
the doorway. The name of the small premises can
just be made out: 'The Cabin'. This unusual shop
was built for Mr E.J. Gregory, who owned the
premises that fronted on to the High Street (52
High Street) and this shop front was added on to
the side.

M. Levi, greengrocer, Harrow Road, Kensal Green, *c.* 1910. This business has been traced back to the 1893 Kelly's Directories when the address was 4 Morris Place, Kensal Green. The property is now known as 784 Harrow Road and was first listed as such in the 1907 Kelly's Directory. Alfred Levi ran these premises as a greengrocers (though he is listed in Kelly's Directory as a coal merchant) until 1936. Mrs Cornish deposited this impressive photograph with the Cricklewood Archive in 1983; she was born at 828 Harrow Road, once called 4 Windsor Cottages.

A postcard view of Station Parade, Willesden Green, *c*. 1910. The firms trading here are, right to left; no. 9, John Arthur Sarson, chemist, pharmacist and optician; no. 8, Parr's Bank Limited (manager, George Carr); no. 7, E. Bales and Co., butchers; no. 6, Frederick Pitt, grocer; no. 5, F. Warren and Co., coal & coke merchants and Harry Bates, picture framer.

Kilburn Lane, *c*. 1910, had shops just over the parish boundary in West Kilburn, now in the City of Westminster. In 1907, the last edition of the Kelly's Directory of Willesden to list the east side of the street, the businesses were: no. 330, Mrs Annie Wheaton, stationer; no. 332, John Boatfield, oilman; no. 334, Harry Walters, grocer, then Portnall Road; no. 336, Charles Rudolph Sigmund, baker; no. 338, Ebenezer Davies, dairy; no. 340, Simmons and Co., butchers. This is where the Directory parts company with the photograph as the butcher here is A.W. Philips.

High Street, Harlesden, *c.* 1920. The Jubilee Clock is on the right. Businesses trading at the time were, from the right: no. 53, Boots Cash Chemists; nos 47–51A, W. Lewis and Co., drapers; no. 45, Northwood and Co., watchmakers; no. 43, Domestic Bazaar Co. Ltd; no. 41, William Robinson and Son, corn dealers; nos 37 & 39, F. W. Woolworth and Co. Ltd, fancy bazaar; nos 33 & 35 Hastings Ltd, house furnishers.

Milton Hersant & Sons butcher's shop, 36 Harlesden High Street, *c.* 1900. The shop was established by Arthur Hersant in February 1889. When he died in April 1936, his obituary in the *Willesden Chronicle* suggested that he may have been the oldest established tradesman in Harlesden. Ten years after these premises were opened, they were rebuilt. Later, a new front was put on to the shop, whereupon Mr Hersant added the figures of cats and pigeons which can be seen adorning the roof.

The post office, Kensal Rise Station, *c.* 1920. The post office at 5 Station Road (now Terrace) was situated on the corner of Linden Avenue. It was run by Mr Henry Sharp from 1899 to 1903 when he was described in the Kelly's Directory firstly as a provision dealer and latterly as a grocer. From 1904 the business was listed as a post office and grocers and Mr Sharp is listed every year up to and including 1939.

Stanley's sweet shop, 251 Chapter Road, *c.* 1920. The shop first appears in the Kelly's Directory of 1906, the owner being listed as a Mrs H.M. Stanley. Presumably Mrs Stanley is one of the ladies pictured in the doorway of the shop, perhaps alongside family members. In 1925 the ownership of the store changed, although the new proprietor, Mr Harry Stone, continued to run it as a confectioners.

EDUCATION

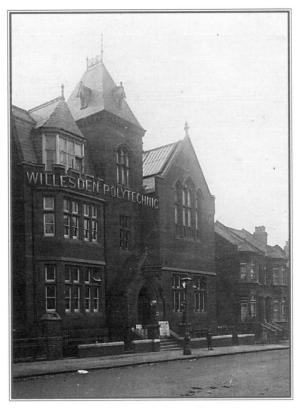

Willesden Polytechnic, c. 1920. In 1896, for the sum of £3,400, Willesden District Council bought the St Lawrence Institute in Priory Park Road. This was to provide the necessary classrooms for Technical Education, urged on by a committee with G.W. Garrett as chair and Stanley Ball as secretary.

St Mary's schools, *c. 1870*. An artistic impression or design for the schools that was unsuccessful. There are a number of differences between this drawing and the building that was erected. Although there are references to a school house as far back as 1686, presumably there was no parish school in 1776 when Richard Freelove left a bequest to erect a village school. Nothing was done until 1809, when the gift was used for its intended purpose. Not all parishioners were happy about providing education: '. . . it is painful to observe that this charitable and wise design has met with considerable opposition from several wealthy farmers in the Parish, who are so nearly allied to the clods they cultivate, as to suppose that even the moderate share of information imparted by an establishment like this must render the children of the poor unfit for useful and contented labour'.

Holy Trinity schools, Canterbury Road, Kilburn, *c. 1935*. A school for 220 boys opened in 1867 in the buildings of St Paul's Church, Kilburn High Road. This school in Canterbury Road, accommodating 440 girls and infants, opened in 1868. The boy's school was closed in 1925 and by 1932 the Canterbury Road site had been reorganized as a boy's school. The council acquired the site in 1937 and the school closed in 1939. It was demolished in the 1950s.

Kilburn Lane, London County Council Board School, *c.* 1890. The poor construction of this school led to an appearance at the Royal Courts of Justice when the London School Board took the builders, Wall Brothers, to court. Above the boys working at carpentry, while below is a 'morning assembly at a Board School'. There are, incredibly, 500 boys in this photograph and the original caption says: 'This band is, all things considered, an excellent one, and its employment conduces greatly to the reverent interest taken by the boys in the proceedings. Prayers, read by the headmaster, follow, after which the scholars go to their respective classrooms to enter upon the studies of the day.'

The Kilburn Grammar School Association Football 1st XI, 1923–4. The school magazine for the Michelmas term 1923 noted: 'We have had some difficulty this season in choosing a team to represent the school in football. Only three of last year's first eleven players remain: Forster (pictured middle, front row), who was elected Captain for the season, Lacey (middle, back row) and Legge (second from left, back row). The rest of the team had to be chosen from last year's 2nd XI.' The team's record from the ten games listed was won three, drew two, lost five.

The nursery school, Lower Place, 1934, In September 1930 Willesden's Director of Education, Mr Davies, wrote to parents, 'Dear Sir or Madam, Nursery Classes for children from 2 to 5 years of age are being opened at Lower Place School. Parents wishing their children to join this Class should fill in the attached slip and return to the Head Teacher.' The *Willesden Chronicle* seemed impressed by this experiment in nursery provision and a lengthy article describing the school and its work appeared in the newspaper on Friday 24 November 1933.

Mora Road Schools, Cricklewood, *c.* 1910. The official opening of these schools took place on Monday 22 July 1907, at 7.30 p.m. The school was described thus: 'This school is erected on a site of about 1½ acre in Mora Road, Cricklewood, and provides accommodation for 1,200 children in separate departments. The Boys' and Girls' Schools for 400 each are arranged in a two storey building, the Girls' being on the ground floor and the Boys on the upper floor. . . . The Infant School for 400 is in a separate one-storey building, and contains a Central Hall . . .8 Class Rooms . . . 2 Cloak Rooms, and 2 Teachers' Rooms. A Caretaker's Residence is also included. Large and airy Playgrounds with Playsheds and Offices are provided. . . . The contract price is £16,726. The Contractors are Messrs W. Lawrence & Son, of Tottenham and Waltham Cross. The picture below is of Class 3, Mora Road, *c.* 1923.

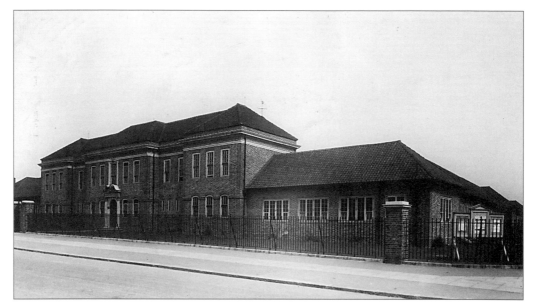

Wykeham School, Aboyne Road, Neasden, *c.* 1930. Its frontage was built within or close to the area of the old Oxgate Prebend. It was named after William of Wykeham, one of the distinguished Prebends of Oxgate and the founder of Winchester School and New College, Oxford. It was officially opened on Friday 17 October 1930 by Morgan Jones, Esq., MP (Parliamentary Secretary to the Board of Education). Among the order of proceedings for the opening ceremony was a rendition of the hymn 'Jerusalem' by the school choir.

Harvist Road or Kensal Rise Boys School, *c.* 1910. The school was opened on 29 August 1898 with 460 boys, their ages ranging from seven to fourteen, and a teaching staff of eight. This photograph purports to show the incorporation of Willesden Teachers Association, on Tuesday 26 September. Unfortunately, there is no year given and the indices at the Cricklewood Archive are unable to fill this omission.

INDUSTRIES &
OCCUPATIONS

Shoot-up-Hill windmill, burnt down in 1863 (see
p. 77). This rare view is taken from Stanley Ball's (see
p. 63) lantern-slide lecture.

Forming part of the Furness family archive, this view shows the Willesden Brick & Tile Works, Chambers Lane and, in the distance, Harrow Hill, in 1928. George Furness, of Roundwood House, was an internationally famous civil works contractor who worked in Italy, France and Brazil, as well as undertaking major railway and other contracts in England. He was also, despite his fierce opposition to its establishment, the first chairman of the Willesden Local Board. His importance to Willesden is currently being re-evaluated and a large collection of maps and plans relating to his building works in Willesden is in the midst of being catalogued. However, there seems little doubt that much archival material that would have shed light on his activities has been lost.

Threatened with demolition in the 1980s although subsequently saved as part of the London Borough of Brent's architectural heritage, this is the New River Water Company pumping station at St Michael's Road, Cricklewood. Located not far from the library (*see* p. 70) and Furness's houses in Larch Road (*see* p. 55), it was built in 1902. Designed by Perry & Co., it is an impressive brick building in the Victorian-Renaissance style, and the chimney stands 135 feet high.

Steam Mill, Shoot-up-Hill, *c.* 1890. The steam mill stood adjacent to the site of the old windmill at the summit of Shoot-up-Hill and fronted directly on to the roadway. Although often assumed to be the successor to the windmill, it was actually erected before that building had burnt down. By the time of this photograph it had become derelict and was subsequently demolished in 1898.

McVitie and Price's Edinburgh biscuit works at Waxlow Road in Park Royal, *c.* 1910. An editorial comment in the *Willesden Chronicle* of 10 November 1905 includes a glowing account of the works and its owner: 'I am indebted to a contemporary for the information that the famous Acton Lane biscuit firm of McVitie and Price has as sole proprietor Mr McVitie . . . . In the building of his factory at Willesden Mr McVitie proved that he could do as much "hustling" as the Americans when occasion demanded . . . . The first sod was cut on 19 November 1901, and by the 9 September 1902, the works were completed, and business there was in full swing.'

Interior and exterior views of the Willesden Council Electricity Department at Salusbury Road in about 1926, as the new showroom was opened on Thursday 9 September 1926. The lower photograph was used in the Willesden Faraday Centenary Handbook and could therefore be closer to the date of September 1931. It seems that it was an urgent demand for better public lighting in Kilburn in about 1895 that led to the council's decision to provide a public supply of electricity. In 1898 a Provisional Order was obtained and the council appointed its first electrical engineer that year. The erection of the generating station at Taylor's Lane followed and in June 1903 the council commenced supplying electricity. However, this state of affairs continued only until 8 February 1904 when negotiations which had commenced in 1902 were brought to a successful conclusion and the council sold its generating station to the North Metropolitan Electric Power Supply Company, who in 1899 had begun work on the power station at Acton Lane (*see* p. 114).

Two views of the forge at Neasden around the turn of the century (above) and in about 1930 (below). The Jackman family was a very old Neasden family connected with the Twyfords (*see* p. 23). Mr Henry George Jackman was the last village blacksmith and it was run by him until it was closed in 1930. The forge, which in Mr Jackman's obituary in the *Willesden Chronicle* is described as '. . . under a spreading chestnut tree . . .' (the one just to the left of the smithy, presumably) had been in the family since 1810. 'During those days as many as five men were employed there and horses came from Kensington, Maida Vale, Kilburn, Wembley, Kingsbury and Harrow to be reshod. On a winter's night when the roads were bad Mr Jackman's assistants would be roughing the smooth shoes until after midnight and a stream of horses would queue down Neasden Lane waiting their turn.' George's brother Frank, owned a number of newsagents and George took over the tobacco and paper shop at Neasden Lane when the smithy closed.

Acton Lane Power Station, Park Royal, *c.* 1920. From *The Engineer* of 4 May 1900 we learn that: 'It possesses extraordinary facilities for obtaining fuel, which can either be brought straight on to the site from the railway – the trucks being taken right underneath a Temperley transport – or on the canal, the barges also being cleared by the transporter. Moreover, the water of the canal is available, and there is hence every opportunity of cheap production. The company is certainly to be congratulated on its choice of site, for beyond these considerations there is the fact that it is sufficiently far removed from private residences to render indictment for any nuisance a practical impossibility.'

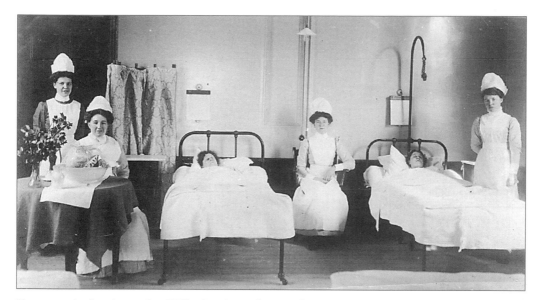

Nurses on the female ward at Willesden General Hospital (*see* p. 74), 1910. Nursing in the eighteenth century was chiefly a menial task, the requirement for being a nurse was: '. . . the length of time she could be kept out of the pothouse'. But between 1893 and 1913 the number of nurses in the country increased over two and a half times. Around the time of this photograph nurses at Willesden Infirmary (*see* p. 72) earned £10 per annum and 5*s* was deducted to pay for their *Science and Art of Nursing* each month and although the training was supposed to last three years, there was in actual fact very little training received.

Works outing, *c.* 1910. This carefully posed photograph is probably of the employees of the Metropolitan Railway Company who later constructed houses for their workers at Aylesbury Street, Neasden (*see* p. 51). While the women and children sit at the middle or to the front of the group, the men stand at the back. There is a minister at the centre right of the picture. The donor, Mr Rose, did suggest that his parents were visible in the photograph but did not leave details as to exactly where.

Willesden dairy men in the 1920s. Above is an unknown dairyman and, perhaps, his son on their rounds while below is Mr Goodchild, leaning against his three-wheeled cart. The firm's name 'Willesden Central Dairies' and their address at Church Road is clearly visible, and so is a large churn and a basket (handle only noticeable) containing eggs. There is also a milk bottle among the metal milk cans. The photograph was taken in Burnley Road, Willesden, by a photographer who used to take photos of local tradesmen once a year or so.

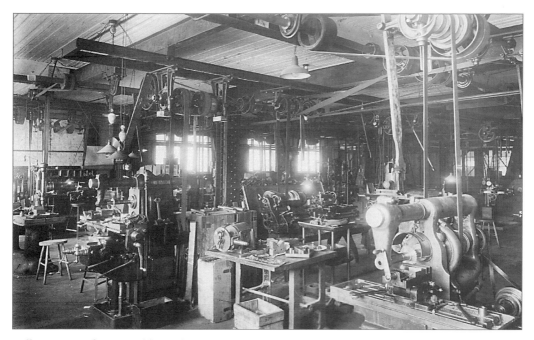

Rolls Razor works at Cricklewood, *c.* 1930. Rolls Razor established their operation at Cricklewood in about 1927. In the top photograph the lathes and polishing machines can be seen while below is the interior of the first aid room with a member of staff undergoing some minor treatment. The photographs come from an exhaustive survey of the firm's activities in the 1930s. During the Second World War, as a war production measure, the company was allowed to extend their premises subject to certain agreements with the council. When the council belatedly required that these agreements be put into force, in April 1961, an angry workforce petitioned the council, arguing that to implement the agreements would lead to redundancies. Eventually the company and the council agreed to an extension of the lease which gave Rolls Razor Limited three years to find alternative accommodation and thus avoid redundancies.

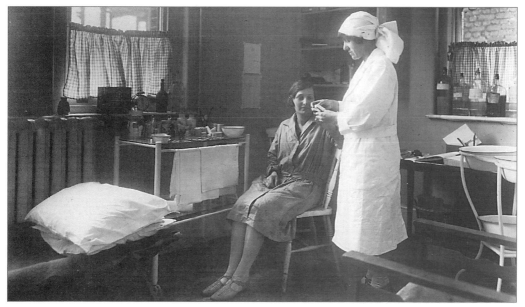

Harlesden post office, 1910. A wonderful photograph of the sorting office erected in Station Road, Harlesden. In 1905 the *Willesden Chronicle* was commenting: 'Rapid progress is being effected with the new sorting office HM Office of Works are erecting in Station Road, Harlesden, and the doubling of the accommodation of the postal staff there is another indication of the enormous growth of Willesden. Messrs Shelbourne and Co., of Fenchurch Street, are undertaking the building of the addition, whose picturesque frontal stone, carved with the King's crown and monogram, E. VII. R., gives the institution a proper official appearance. The massive semi-circular front window is of Bath stone, and similar stone is being used in the dressing of the other parts of the building, the pediment, and the entrance.'

Beeson's premises, High Street, Harlesden, *c.* 1890. The Beeson family were active in local affairs and their forge in the High Street eventually evolved into the rather elaborate premises above. A great many details can be found on this image, such as the blacksmiths at work in the forge and the table lamps in the window.

WARTIME

*A formal portrait of George Hebb Taylor (1890–1977) in full
military uniform and wearing his medals. The photograph was
taken by J. Glass of Londonderry, around the time of the First
World War. Mr Taylor lived at 3 Craven Park Road, Harlesden for
a number of years.*

Dollis Hill House hospital, 1916 (above). This intriguing photo was found in the visitors book when it was donated (Acc. 242/1977). The photograph clearly shows the staff of the war hospital, apparently including the room service personnel, although just what their particular role was is a little unclear. Dollis Hill House was a convalescent and open air hospital for sick and wounded soldiers, an Auxiliary Hospital (Class 'A') attached to the Endell Street Military Hospital. The first patients were received on Monday 14 February and within a week, every bed was occupied. Below is seen The Grove, Neasden when it too was in use as a war hospital. The Grove Military Hospital, Neasden, next to St Catherine's, was opened by Mr and Mrs Glanfield on 15 December 1914 for the use of the Reserve Battalion of the IXth Middlesex Regiment. It began with just six beds, kindly lent by several Neasden ladies. Apparently, as this picture shows, the convalescents greatly appreciated the free use of the gardens where they amused themselves playing croquet and clock golf. Surgeon Captain Muller was the regimental doctor who visited on a daily basis or more frequently when required.

The Drill Hall, Pound Lane, *c.* 1914. This is the Drill Hall, Pound Lane, the plans for which were passed by the Council on 20 December 1910. The architect was Sydney W. Cranfield Esq., 14 South Square, Gray's Inn, WC, and the letter from O. Claude Robson referred to '. . .your plan for the headquarters of the IX Battalion DCO Middlesex Regiment, Pound Lane.' There was a long and protracted correspondence after the Drill Hall was completed due to the unmade-up state of Pound Lane, the problems concerning the height of the curbs and the fixing of the boundaries between the Council's property and that of the War Office. It is a sad fact that this impressive and imposing site has been all but obscured by the addition of new buildings.

The remains of the bus in which two local men died during the First World War, in 1915. 'Killed on duty in the air raid of 13 October, and who, as we reported last week, were accorded a public funeral at Cricklewood. The Revd. T.D. Lloyd, vicar of St Michael's, Cricklewood, urged that it was the duty of Englishmen to avenge the lives of these innocent victims of German hatred. He appealed to the manhood of the nation never to sheath the sword and never to cease fighting until the demon of blood and carnage had been crushed. Rogers and Tarrant, he said, had died at the post of duty, as true heroes as those who perished on the field of battle.'

It would be misleading, in providing an example of the usual images held in the London Borough of Brent's archive, if there were not at least one of which little or nothing is known. This magnificent, striking image, which presumably dates from the First World War era, is the example chosen for this book. The quality of the image is delightful, and it is all the sadder therefore, that we are unable to place these gentlemen in their correct historical and geographical context. Look at the definition on the faces of the players and coaches. Such is the quality of this photograph that it is a welcome addition to the archive. If only we knew more . . .

An air raid shelter at The Circle, Neasden, *c.* 1940. This picture was donated by a member of the ARP party in 1978 and among the wardens pictured are B. Northcutt, Grunguist, Kynaston and Fidgen. During the Second World War there were over 1,000 air raid warnings in Willesden; 572 high explosive and parachute mines were dropped and 19 flying bombs and rockets landed.

ARP wardens pictured outside the ARP Centre in Gladstone Park (known as the Hub) in early 1940. The photograph was donated by Mr S. 'Tommy' Shapps who is seated on the front row, far left. The other people whom he identified in the picture include Tommy Smith (shift leader), far right, front row and 'Tubby' Wright, middle row, fifth from the left.

Two postwar photographs sent to the archive by the Public Relations Office at the Town Hall, Wembley. Above is the interior of a prefab that was an ex-army hut at The Drive, Gladstone Park, *c.* 1947. The end walls are brick with a corrugated iron section making up the other walls and the roof. The stove at the right of the picture provided the heating and was, of course, used for cooking. There is linoleum on the floor and the woman in the picture is standing next to a cabinet that is stocked with groceries. Below is a prefab with a very well maintained garden. The occupants are seen tending the plot which is well stocked with plants; a small boy rides his tricycle on the path. This could well be one of the prefabs that were sited around Gladstone Park and provided emergency accommodation after the 1939–45 war.

ACKNOWLEDGEMENTS

I feel it is important to acknowledge the many donations to the museum and archive, both documented and anonymous, that have enabled me to produce this work. I should also like to acknowledge a personal debt to the many organizations and individuals, both within the Brent Council and beyond, who have helped in this venture. In particular I would like to thank Bridget Keane, Ian Johnston and Cliff Wadsworth for their time and effort, Christie, Karen and Cathy for their patience and all at the Grange Museum for their support.

On a personal level I should like to acknowledge a debt to my family, Lorraine, Laura and James for their continual love, encouragement and support. Finally thanks to Paul (just back from Oz) for not helping in any way.

BIBLIOGRAPHY

Corporation of Willesden, *The Willesden Survey 1949*, London 1950

Dewe, D. and Sanson, A., *From Bacon Lane to Yuletide Road: A Guide to Brent Street Names*, London, Brent Library Service, 1975

Leff, V. and Blunden, G.H., *Willesden Story*, London, Pitman, 1962

Victoria History of the Counties of England: Middlesex, Vol. VII, Oxford University Press, 1982 (Willesden)

Willesden (and *Brent*) *Chronicle*

INDEX

To order any of these titles please telephone our distributor, Littlehampton Book Services on 01903 721596
For a catalogue of these and our other titles please ring Regina Schinner on 01453 731114